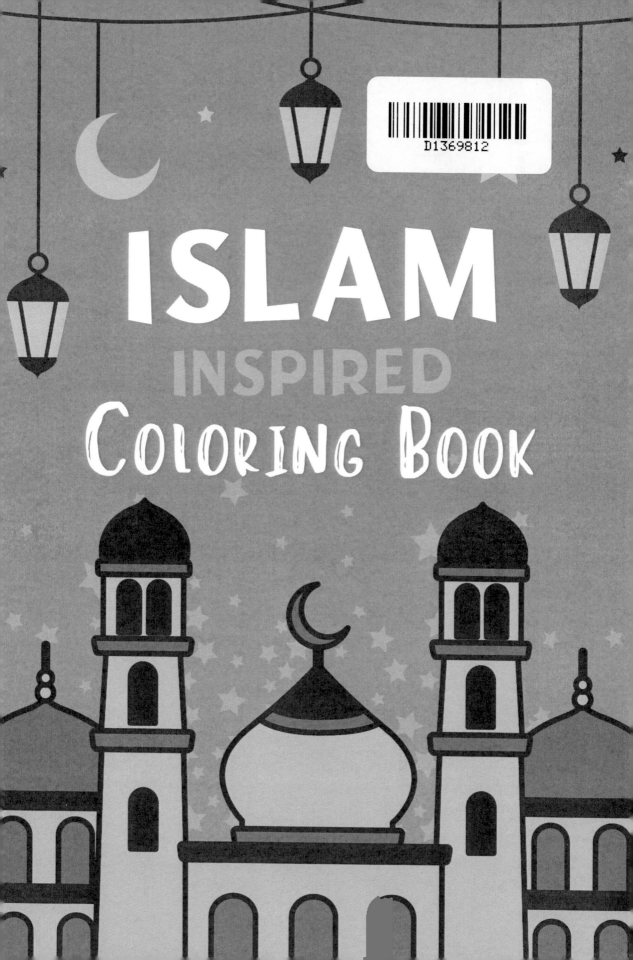

ISLAM
INSPIRED
Coloring Book

اَلسَّلَامُ عَلَيْكُمْ وَرَحْمَةُ اللّٰهِ وَ بَرَكَاتُهُ

Assalamo alaikum wa
rahmatullahe wa barakatohu.

Peace be on you and the
mercy and blessings of Allah.

بِسْمِ اللّٰهِ الرَّحْمٰنِ الرَّحِيْم

Bismillahir Rahmanir Raheem.In the name
of Allah, the Gracious, the Merciful.

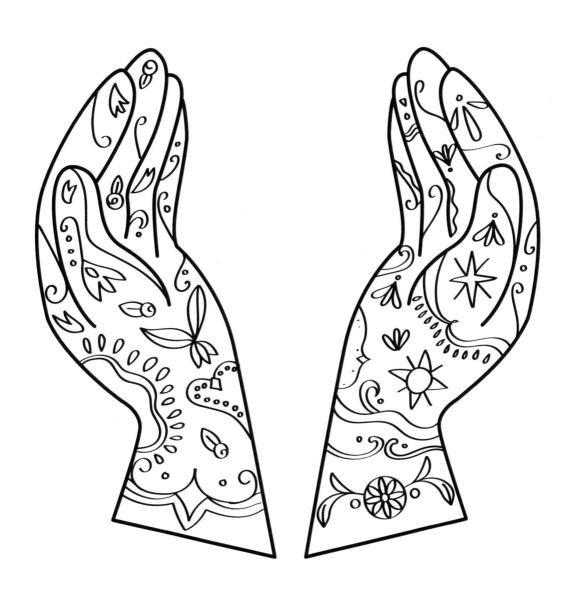

رَبِّ زِدْنِيْ عِلْمًا

Rabbe zidni ilma.O

Lord, increase my knowledge.

بِسْمِ اللَّهِ الرَّحْمَٰنِ الرَّحِيمِ

سُبْحَانَ رَبِّىَ الْاَعْلٰى

Subhana Rabbe yal Aa'la.

Glory to my Lord the most High.

سُبْحَانَ اللّٰهِ ـ اَلْحَمْدُ لِلّٰهِ ـ اَللّٰهُ اَكْبَرْ

Subhaan Allah, Alhamdo lillah, Allaho Akbar.

Glory to Allah, all praise belongs to Allah,

Allah is the Greatest.

اَلْحَمْدُ لِلّٰهِ

Alhamdo lillah.

All praise belongs to Allah.

اَعُوْذُ بِاللّٰهِ مِنَ الشَّيْطٰنِ الرَّجِيْمِ

Aaoozobillahe minushaitanir rajeem.

I seek refuge with Allah from Satan, the accursed.

اَللّٰهُ اَكْبَرْ

Allaho akbar.

Allah is the Greatest.

سُبْحَانَ رَبِّيَ الْأَعْلَى

سُبْحَانَ اللّٰهِ

Subhaan Allah.

Glory to Allah.

EID Mubarak

وَعَلَيْكُمُ السَّلَام

Wa alaikum salaam.

And peace be on you too.